# ON THE MOVE...

# CUSTOM CYCLES

## By Mark Rich

CHILDRENS PRESS, CHICAGO

Library of Congress Cataloging in Publication Data

Rich, Mark J
  Custom cycles.

  (On the move)
  SUMMARY: Discusses ways to customize a stock
motorcycle, including modifying the engine for
extra speed.
  1. Motorcycles—Juvenile literature.
2. Motorcycles—Customizing—Juvenile literature.
[1. Motorcycles—Customizing. 2. Motorcycles]
I. Title.
TL440.R47     629.2′275     80-26659
ISBN 0-516-03887-7

Picture Acknowledgements

Mark Rich—2, 4, 5, 6, 7, 8, 9, 10, 12, 14, 15, 16,
  20, 21, 22, 23, 24, 25, 26, 27, 28, 29, 30, 31, 32,
  34, 35, 36, 37, 38, 39, 40, 41, 42, 43
Photos courtesy of *Rider* magazine, copyrighted
TL Enterprises, Inc.- 17, 18, COVER

  The author wishes to gratefully acknowledge
help and cooperation of the following: Bertram
terprises, Glendale, Arizona; Joe Livesay, Ba
Barrett, Kerry Reed, Bruce Golden, Ed Leveg
Highway Choppers, Glendale, Arizona; No
Bruce and Bruce Vickerman of Performance Fo
Phoenix, Arizona; Stan Lumpp of City Suzu
BMW, Glendale, Arizona Jack Lanley,
Monaghan and Group Promotions in associat
with the International Championship Auto Sh
series.
  Without the help of these people and organi
tions, this book would not have been possi
Thanks to them all.

Many companies make motorcycles. Some are British; some are German; others are Japanese and Swedish. Here are a few cycle companies: Kawasaki, Yamaha, Harley-Davidson, Triumph, Suzuki, BMW, and Honda. There are more! Each of these companies makes from a few to a whole slew of different two-wheeled machines.

A motorcycle that is equipped like it is from the factory with no extras or specially made parts or any fancy stuff is called a "stock" cycle.

Any stock motorcycle can be made into a custom machine. Usually, though, a nice, new stock motorcycle stays that way for a good long time if treated properly.

This real old-timer is in "cherry" (super) condition. It is a 1947 Indian "Chief." There are about 8000 original miles on this machine!

All the parts and equipment on this 60-inch wheelbase cycle are original (the ones it came with when it was brand new).

Its engine has a 73.625 cubic inch displacement, deep-finned, high-compression aluminum cylinder heads with bronze spark plug inserts, and a three-speed transmission. It's an "oldie but goodie."

In the United States, engines are rated by the cubic inch (cu. in.) method. In Japan and Europe, engines are sized according to cubic centimeters (cc).

Whether you're talking cc's or cubic inches, you're referring to the volume of space inside the engine's cylinders. The more volume, the bigger the engine and the more power it can put out.

Engines on stock motorcycles start around 90cc for the smaller bikes and proceed up to 1200cc or more on the really big machines.

A basic 1000cc four-cycle (also called four stroke), four-cylinder Honda engine powers this machine.

A four-cycle engine has pistons that move up and down in the cylinders four times to complete all the jobs they do.

First comes the intake stroke. The piston moves down in the cylinder and the fuel/air mixture enters. Number 2 stroke is compression. The piston moves up in the cylinder and squeezes the air/gas at the top. Third is the power stroke. The air/gas is ignited by the spark plug and the piston is sent shooting down in the cylinder. The last stroke is the exhaust stroke. The piston moves back up toward the top of the cylinder and the exhaust is shoved out.

Some motorcycles come equipped with six-cylinder engines. It takes a pretty strong rider to roll and control a heavy Honda like this. It weighs around 650 pounds.

A six-cylinder engine powers this maroon two-wheeler. The exhaust header pipes head out of each side of the front of the engine. The pipes turn back toward the back wheel, and gather at the muffler and exhaust pipe.

This is the case to a motorcycle engine. The two cylinders will anchor over those two large holes with the four bolts that stick up around each one. Rods will go down through those holes. The rods connect the pistons in the cylinders to the crankshaft and flywheel down in the case.

In the picture at the right, the engine case is going to be worked on. The rough edges will be taken off and the holes smoothed out.

The piston (on the left) goes up and down inside the cylinder (on the right). The piston fits very tightly inside the cylinder. Steel rings fit around the top of the piston in those grooves. The rings hold the piston in the cylinder even tighter.

The piston is attached by rods to the crankshaft. The piston going up and down in the cylinder turns the crankshaft. The crankshaft moves the chain or belt drive, and that makes the rear wheel turn.

9

Some motorcycles have next-to-nothing (or nothing!) as far as instrumentation goes.

The Honda six-cylinder bike has a number of gauges and lights that let the rider know how the machine is working.

The large dial, top left, is the speedometer. Speed is calibrated (measured) in both miles per hour and kilometers per hour. The odometer is there, too. This records the distance the bike has traveled.

The top number shows the total number of miles the machine has traveled. The bottom number is a trip odometer. A rider can re-set it each time to check the total miles traveled on any trip.

The small dial in the center of the pack has the information on the volts working in your machine's electrical system. If everything's OK, the needle points pretty well dead center (when the engine's on). Too far to the left and the electrical system is undercharging. Too far right and the system is overcharging.

The large dial on the far right is the tachometer ("tach"). It tells how fast the engine is going, or the RPMs (Revolutions Per Minute). You multiply the numbers it has printed on its dial by 1000. So, if the tach needle reads a 4, your engine's turning 4000 RPMs. That means the drive shaft of your bike is making 4000 complete turns in one minute!

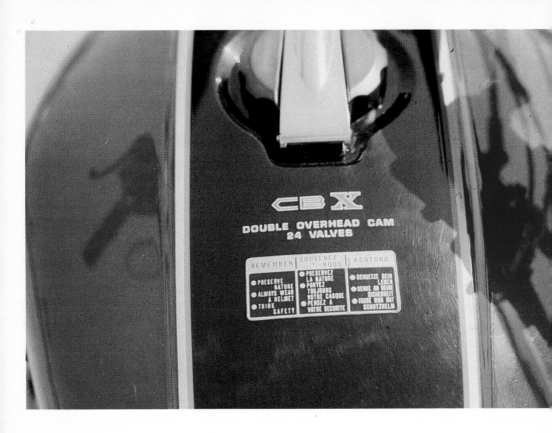

The gas tank of this six-cylinder cycle has quite a bit of information.

Double overhead cams and 24 valves mean basically this: A valve is a covering of an opening in the top of a cylinder. Gas and air go into the cylinders through the holes the valves cover up. Exhaust leaves the cylinders through other holes that the valves cover.

A cam, or camshaft, is a sturdy metal rod that turns and lets different valves open and close at the times they're supposed to. "Double Overhead Cam" means there are two cams and they are along the top part of the engine.

So, in a nutshell, all that means is that the bike has 24 ports (holes) in the engine (four for each cylinder) and 24 valves cover them up. The bike has two camshafts that are in the top part of the engine and those two shafts open and close the 24 valves.

Can you read the rest of the decal? The first third is in English. The second is French, and the last is German. Whatever language you use, it's all the same good cycling advice! Wearing safety glasses to protect your eyes is good advice, too.

There are different types of motorcycle frames. One type is called "rigid;" another is the "swingarm" frame.

With a rigid frame, like the bike has here, the back wheel is anchored securely to the non-moving one-piece main frame.

With a swingarm arrangement, the rear wheel is attached to a moveable back section of frame. This moveable back section has a shock-absorbing, cushioning effect on the ride.

14

This 1969 cycle is called a "shovel head." That may sound strange to you, but it's called that for a good reason.

The "head" of an engine is the top part, where the valves and tops of the cylinders are. The heads have covers over them to protect the parts underneath.

So you figure it out. What shape do you think the head covers are on this Harley (Harley-Davidson motorcycle)?

This 1977 cycle has two quite-noticeable features. First are the handlebars. They have been set atop risers. Risers are used to raise the handlebar mounting point above its usual location, thus giving a higher appearance.

The second noticeable thing is the disc brake rotor. Some cycles have drum, others have disc brakes. A disc brake uses pads pushing on a disc (called a rotor) to stop the machine.

At times, discs on motorcycles have holes drilled through them. The holes help cool, keep water from collecting on, lighten, and fancy-up a disc.

Some bikers ride solo (by themselves). Maybe they have somewhere they need to go, so they take their cycles. Perhaps they just want to get out on the road and cruise. Whatever the reason, they hop on their bikes and take off.

Some cyclists are so into their cycles that they don't own a car or truck or any other form of transportation. One biker said, "Hey, the only reason to have a four-wheeled cage (a car or truck) is to haul your cycle around anyway!"

Many bikers belong to clubs or other groups that ride places together. Sometimes only a few head out on a hundred or many-hundred mile journey. At other times, ten or twenty or more bikes and riders show up and participate in making the trip.

You just can't stop real bike enthusiasts. They figure out a way to keep on rolling!

Some cycles are completely stock.
Other bikes are customized. Sometimes the
changes are small. But often a cycle is so
customized that there is hardly a thing on it
that was part of the original equipment.

This red 1965 "solo" machine is pretty
much stock, believe it or not. Back when it
was made, it had similar whitewall tires,
the luggage rack, saddlebags with guards,
and a windshield. The main custom item
on this machine now is an "S & S Super"
carburetor, installed to improve the
engine's performance.

The red bike on the last page and this
blue one are very similar 1965 machines.
They both have the 74 cubic inch (1200cc)
two-cylinder, four cycle engine. They are both
Harley-Davidson cycles. They are both
"panheads." A "panhead" bike has engine
head covers that are shaped like pie pans.

Many original non-chrome parts of this
blue cycle are now chrome-plated. When
you get parts of your machine chromed,
you take them to a shop where they do
chrome plating. The workers there
securely bond a layer of chromium metal to
the surface of that part and presto! Shine
City!

Two straight custom pipes, one from each cylinder, lead back toward the rear of this bike.

A straight pipe, also called a "drag" pipe, has no muffler. With no muffler, a cycle's engine will sound off pretty loud and clear, which is exactly what some bikers want! They're proud of their bikes and don't mind letting others know they're coming along the street! This biker even has a demon painted on his cycle.

Some motorcycles are customized only for SPEED!

This 903 cc was hefted up to a 1105cc, turbocharged, and modified in a number of other ways. It has hit 153.58 miles per hour in the quarter mile for its fastest speed to date. It had a 9.40 ET (Elapsed Time—the time it took the machine to cover the quarter-mile strip) for its fastest time. Any way you want to look at it, that's moving!

Sometimes in racing, a machine's fastest time (ET) is not its fastest speed (Miles Per Hour). That may sound sort of funny, but it's the truth!

You'll notice all the hardware on this baby is slung really low to the ground. The lower the parts are, the lower the center of gravity of the machine. The lower the center of gravity, the easier the driver can balance it.

In addition, with racing cycles, you want to keep a low profile (not be stuck way up in the air). With a low profile, air and wind will have less of a chance to push against you and your bike, so you can go faster.

Supercharging helps increase the horsepower of a motorcycle. Engine power can be increased up to 60 percent with the proper supercharging equipment.

On the right side of the cycle is the air intake and blower unit. The thing that looks like a cigar box with ridged sides and four screws in the top sucks in air. The rounded metal structure under the air intake is the blower, which forces the air and fuel that has been mixed with it into the engine.

On the left side of the cycle you'll find the belt drive that supplies the power to the blower. The belt and pulleys it goes over are toothed so the belt won't slip and blower power won't be lost.

At the drags, before driving up to the
starting line, bikers drive into a water
puddle—on purpose! The driver steadies
his back tire in the puddle, puts the bike in
gear, and lets the back wheel spin like
mad. It's called a "burn out"!

A burn out gets the tire rubber hot and
sort of gummy so when the race begins, the
back wheel will grab the road really well.
A burn out's a traction helper.

Bikes and cars that are slated to race at the drags need to go through time trials. Time trials help the drivers see how their machines are running, give them a warm-up, and qualify them for a certain "bracket" or division to race in later for prizes.

Since many vehicles and drivers may be at a drag strip to race, everyone has to line up and wait his turn.

At a custom motorcycle shop, you can find all sorts of snazzy parts and goodies for your bike. You can go "all the way" and have so many added and changed parts that the bike would hardly be recognizable as whatever brand and model it was to start with.

Most custom bikes start with a used engine and an old frame (or one specially built). Then custom parts are added according to the builder's fancy.

There are many chain guards, front forks, seats, handlebars, fenders, and loads of other things to give your cycle the look you want. With custom cycles, after all, you won't find any two exactly alike.

Work is in progress, on building a
custom bike from the ground floor up. The
frame, back wheel, engine, and tank are in
place.

Since the motorcycle's custom, probably
none of those parts are from the same
original machine. In fact, many parts on a
custom cycle are made from scratch and
were never on a regular stock motorcycle
before at all!

A large number of machines and tools, big and small, are used to work on customizing and repairing motorcycles.

The red piece of hardware here has many functions. It smooths the insides of engine cylinders, rebuilds rods (pencil-shaped metal engine parts), and shapes and smooths other metal motor parts so they fit and work like they're supposed to.

A skilled mechanic carefully uses that precision machine to smooth out the insides of a cylinder. A fine oil is circulated up into where the inside cylinder metal is being honed down. The oil helps to lubricate the machinery as it works, to cut down on the heat build-up with the metal cutting, and to allow the work to go smoothly.

Some folks just don't have the time or expensive machinery to do all the work on their engines themselves. So they take their cycle engines into a shop and have them rebuilt, overhauled, or whatever!

Now, people don't normally yank the engines out of their motorcycles and bring them in for work. They usually bring in the whole bike—it's easier!

This engine's probably waiting for some guy who's working on putting a custom cycle together himself. He's undoubtedly welding, sanding, painting, and doing all sorts of things to the rest of the motorcycle, preparing it for the engine that's all wrapped up waiting for him at the shop!

All sorts of work is done on custom motorcycles. The front end maintenance on this machine could be something as easy as fixing a flat tire, or as hard as straightening the fork that holds the front wheel.

Since most motorcycles have a side kickstand, sort of like your own bicycle does, when the front wheel's off, there's one slight problem: How do you keep the cycle standing up?

No sweat! Just lift her up on a steel crate and you're in business!

This man had a lot of work to do to get his bike the way he wanted it.

For $400, he bought a beat up 900cc cycle. He took it apart (stripped it), had a different frame, front fork, tires, and other extras added. He modified the engine to a beefier 1000cc.

He put a lot of bucks into his machine, of course, but now has a bike he can be proud of. If he sold it, he could probably get somewhere around $2500 for it! But it's not for sale!

Not counting time, labor, and sweat, this machine's worth about $11,000! The push rod tubes, horn, braided cables, rear wheel hub, and some other accessories are 24-carat gold! A number of other parts are chromed, too. Just look at that shine!

The owner has built some of the bike's parts by hand. The chain guard and "sissy" bar on the back end were made by hand.

Most of the time there are spokes connecting the rim to the hub with motorcycle wheels.

Spokes need to be straight, strong, and aligned properly so the wheels they're holding don't vibrate or collapse at high speeds.

The front wheel on this Harley is spoked, but it has a chromed wheel cover to give it a custom look. You won't see too many cycles around with that sort of set-up!

An upturned rear fender finishes out the custom work on a cream-colored motorcycle.

Fenders on cycles don't just sit there and look good, you know. They are there for a reason. When a bike plows through water, mud, dirt, or sand, all that stuff goes flying. Some of it sticks to the tires as they spin and flies up toward the driver. Fenders protect the rider.

See how the pinstriping lines on the tank and the frame go together? A sharp-looking tank adds a lot to the overall appearance of a motorcycle.

Much time, effort, and skill go into making a custom-detailed gas tank. It must first be sanded down to bare metal. Then a primer coat or two of paint is applied. Next comes the finishing coat or coats with the personalized striping or other art work. Last, the final coats of lacquer are sprayed on. Sometimes ten, fifteen, or more final coats are sprayed on for that high-gloss shine!

A custom street bike with this style is called a chopper. A chopper describes a motorcycle that has been stripped down. All unnecessary items (fenders, chrome) have been taken off.

The seat, engine, and frame are often lower than what you'd find on a stock bike. The front fork on a chopper is usually longer than a standard fork, too. It reaches way out in front of the machine to give the rider a sort of "kick-back" look.

This chopper style motorcycle has a "springer" front end. With a springer, one fork comes down from the handlebars to hold the front wheel securely. A second fork is also attached to the front wheel. At the top of the second fork are shock absorbers—they look like springs.

When a bike with a springer front end hits a bump, that second fork with the shock-absorbing springs takes up some of the jolt and the bike and biker cruise along in comfort.

At a custom car, truck, and cycle show, most entries are roped off so people won't touch the chrome, the paint jobs, or the engines. People don't mean to, but sometimes that constant touching and rubbing can make a shiny machine not-so-shiny or even damage paint or engine work.

Mirrors are placed beneath machines so that the undercarriage, special paint, chrome, or machinery of the vehicle can be seen. At a custom show everything must be spotless!

Specifications ("specs") for cycles, cars, and other entries at a custom vehicle show are given on cards that are placed around the machines. The information given on these cards is such things as year, make and model of the machine, engine size, drive train modifications, name of owner, the names of people who did the custom paint work, striping, engine work, and more!

This is a good, heavy highway bike. It has a 1200cc engine, which is almost as powerful as a Volkswagen Beetle's engine, and the Beetle has LOTS more weight to push around, too!

"Saddlebags" on either side of the rear wheel make it easy to carry things rather than having to hold them with one hand and attempt to drive with the other.

The engine of a VW is, many times, the power plant of a custom motor trike. Volkswagen engines are small and strong and there are plenty of places that carry parts for them, so they're a good bet!

A VW engine is four-cylinder, air-cooled, and adapts nicely to a three-wheeler.

The power pack of this blue "trike" (short for tricycle) is the same as the ones found in VW Bugs.

A lot of work goes into a machine like this one. Creations like it have to be made pretty much from scratch. It's an original, a one-of-a-kind.

You could call it a trike, a three-wheel motorcycle, a cycle, a three-seater motor bike, or a lot of other things, but the owner has named it "Jay's Distorted Pumpkin!"

About forty horsepower from a VW engine push this three-wheeler along the street. Besides having three wheels, this carrot-orange beauty can haul three passengers.

## FACTS ABOUT MOTORCYCLE ACCIDENTS

- When a driver and passenger are involved in a motorcycle accident their chances of being injured or killed are greater than if they were riding in a vehicle with more protection.
- Studies show that most of the motorcycle operators involved in accidents are young—under 20.
- The majority of accidents take place during daylight hours.
- All studies show that the head, arm, and leg are the parts of the body most often injured.
- The most serious type of injury occurs to the head.

## MOTORCYCLE SAFETY FACTS

- Some states require that motorcycle riders wear protective helmets. Other states do not have a helmet law. Still the smart driver and passenger will, for safety's sake, wear helmets whenever riding on a motorcycle.
- Wear a helmet with a face shield or safety goggles to protect your eyes.
- Wearing a long-sleeve jacket, long pants, leather gloves, and sturdy shoes will further protect the body in case of an accident.
- Consider every road a potential obstacle course and drive defensively.
- Keep your head up and your eyes moving so you can anticipate hazards ahead of time.
- Take the path of least resistance and go around rather than over obstacles.
- Slow down before you reach an obstacle.
- Make yourself visible to others. Ride with headlights on at all times, wear bright colored reflective clothing.

# GLOSSARY

**Battery:** a device that makes electricity by chemical action.

**Bearing:** a surface designed to reduce friction between moving parts. Roller and ball-shaped bearings are examples.

**Brake:** a device that applies friction to halt or slow down anything in motion.

**Cam:** a disk or cylinder with an irregular shape so that its motion, usually rotary, gives to other parts or part in contact with it a special motion as well.

**Carburetor:** engine part that mixes fuel with air, vaporizes the fuel and air and sends it on to cylinders.

**Center of gravity:** the point (sometimes outside of the object) at which an object could be suspended so the entire weight would be balanced. For example, mobiles hang from their center of gravity.

**Chopper:** term used for stripped down motorcycle from which all unnecessary items have been removed.

**Chrome plate:** to plate (cover) with chromium, a shiny, silver-colored metal. Chromium is used in alloys and electroplating to increase strength and prevent corrosion.

**Crankshaft:** a shaft having angled parts. Pistons are attached to the crankshaft by rods. These rods push down on the crankshaft to make it turn.

**Cubic measurement:** measurement having three dimensions; measures volume or space using inches or centimeters. For example, a cubic inch is one inch high, one inch wide, and one inch deep.

**Customized** or **custom-made:** something made specially for an individual, made to special order.

**Cylinder:** a chamber in an engine in which the pressure of a gas or liquid moves a sliding piston.

**Elapsed time:** time it takes for a vehicle to travel a specific distance. Time measure used in motorcycle races.

**Engine:** a machine that burns fuel to make a vehicle move. Engines convert energy into mechanical work.

**Exhaust pipe:** pipes used to let the steam or gases from the cylinder of an engine escape.

**Fenders:** a part mounted over the wheels to protect the rider from splashing of mud or water.

**Horsepower:** unit of power defined as 746 watts or 550 foot-pounds per second.

**Internal-combustion engine:** engine in which fuel is burned inside a cylinder.

**Kilometer:** unit of measurement of length. 1 kilometer equals 1000 meters or 3280.8 feet or 0.621 mile.

**Mile:** unit of distance equal to 5280 feet or 1760 yards.

**Muffler:** a device used to deaden sound of the escaping gases in an internal-combustion engine.

**Odometer:** gauge that measures how far a vehicle has traveled; shows distance traveled.

**Panhead:** engine head cover shaped like a pan.

**Piston:** closely fitted sliding piece (usually cylindrical in shape) which is moved or moves against the pressure of a liquid or a gas without allowing escape of fluid. The piston compresses the fuel and air, in the cylinder.

**RPM:** revolutions per minute.

**Saddlebags:** pair of bags hung over back wheels of motorcycle.

**Shock absorber:** hydraulic piston that absorbs energy from springs.

**Shovelhead:** engine head cover shaped like a shovel.

**Solo:** alone.

**Spark plug:** in an internal-combustion engine the electrical device that produces a spark in the cylinder, thus causing the air-fuel mixture to ignite.

**Speedometer:** a gauge that shows how many miles or kilometers per hour a vehicle is traveling.

**Stock motorcycle:** a cycle manufactured by a factory. A stock cycle that has not been changed in any way.

**Tachometer:** instrument that counts the number of revolutions or the velocity of a rotating shaft, records in rpm.

**Tank:** container holding a liquid or gas.

**Traction:** contact between the wheels and pavement provides hold for the wheels.

**Tricycle:** a three-wheeled motorcycle.

**Turbo-charged:** engine with increased power, often uses a device to increase the power by adding a compressor or blower to force more fuel and air into the cylinder than would normally be drawn in by the piston.

**Valve:** any device for opening or closing the flow of liquid, gas, or other material through a specific space.

**Volts:** quality of electrical potential difference; one volt is potential difference across a conductor having a resistance of one ohm which makes a current of one ampere.

## INDEX

**About The Author:**

Mark Rich was born November 23, 1948 in Ray, Arizona, a small copper-mining company town. In 1952, the family moved to the Los Angeles, California area. He attended elementary and high school in the Los Angeles suburbs, and in 1966, began studies in Arizona State University in Tempe. He received a B.A. in Elementary Education from Arizona State in 1970 and an M.A. in Elementary Education from the same institution in 1972. He is currently finishing his 8th year of teaching in Phoenix, Arizona. He has taught 4th, 5th, and 6th grades.

 His hobbies include traveling, writing, stereo, tennis, golf, and photography.